JOURN
DRIVERS
OF ATHLETIC SUCCESS
What Every Athlete Needs to Know about Peak Performance

MW01490669

DRIVERS

DRIVERS

Foyle Press
PO BOX 589
Orinda California 94563
www.foyle31.com

Ordering Information:
Quantity sales. Special discounts are available on quantity purchases by corporations, associations, and others. For details, contact the publisher at the address above.

Printed in the United States of America

Published by Realization Press

DRIVERS

STEP 1: OWNERSHIP

This journal is DRIVEN by:

_____

(Participants name)

DRIVERS

IMPORTANCE AND BENEFITS OF JOURNALING

Journaling is a very important skill every athlete should develop. It is an essential element in increasing your mental aptitude, not to mention that there are numerous benefits of journaling including reflection, controlling your emotions, improving communication skills, learning to write and reflect on your goals, building your self-confidence, and helping you cope with anxiety and stress. Additionally, journaling helps you track progress, improves discipline, brings your goals into focus, exercises your brain muscles, helps put ideas into words, and improves self-awareness. In your athletic journey you will discover a plethora of personal benefits that may emerge from your journaling experience.

According to Serena Williams, winner of 23 Grand Slam tennis titles, "Writing down your feelings in a notebook or journal can help clear out negative thoughts and emotions that keep you feeling stuck."

I recommend writing in your journal right after a game when you have a moment. Write for about five to ten minutes. It is important that you journal when the game or practice is still fresh in your mind so you can capture minute details about your experience.

Starting a sport journal can be challenging for many people because you don't always know what to write. You might even think it's silly. But journaling is about gaining awareness about your performance but more importantly about the things you need to work on to improve your game. The more you do it the more comfortable it will become. There is an additional benefit of journaling: it can serve as your black book of secrets about your opponent. But ultimately your journal is a guide to your athletic journey; both the good and the bad. It's a journey into discovering your authentic self.

Since journaling can be somewhat difficult to start, here are a few ways to start journaling: write about your favorite basketball or football player. For example:

My favorite basketball player is_____ .

The three things I admire most about my favorite basketball player are:

1. _____

2. _____

3. _____

DRIVERS

IMPORTANCE AND BENEFITS
OF JOURNALING

The three things my favorite basketball player does that I want to be able to do are:

1. _____

2. _____

3. _____

The reasons I love to play basketball are: _____

_____

_____ .

The most fun thing about basketball this year is: _____

_____

_____ .

The funniest thing that ever happened to me playing basketball was: _____

_____

_____ .

The weirdest thing that has ever happened during playing basketball was: _____

_____

_____ .

DRIVERS

IMPORTANCE AND BENEFITS OF JOURNALING

Another way to start your journaling journey is by using it to evaluate your game or contemplate your practice performance.

The following is a template to use to evaluate your game or practice performance:

Performance evaluation suggestions for your journal writing:

Date _____ Opponent _____

Rating My Performance - scale 1-10   (1 being low and 10 being high)

1. ___ My pre-game preparation in regard to water, diet, and sleep.
2. ___ Evaluation of my warm-up.
3. ___ My effort and work rate level.
4. ___ My communication with my teammates.
5. ___ My level of focus.
6. ___ My decision-making under pressure.
7. ___ My goals for the game.
8. ___ My quality of self-talk.
9. ___ Level of integrity with myself.
10. ___ The quality of visualization.
11. ___ Level of emotional control.
12. ___ Level of self-confidence.

Parts of my game that were good today: _____

_____

_____ .

IMPORTANCE AND BENEFITS OF JOURNALING

What I'd like to improve on this week in practice: _____

_____

_____ .

I rate my overall performance today as: _____ .

After you have mastered the art of your journaling experience, don't be afraid to chart your own course, writing about what is important to you as an athlete for your development. I journal a great deal about my public versus my private self and how different they are. I also journal about my fears, hopes, goals, and values. The important thing is to make your journaling experience uniquely yours.

This journal is your private retreat; a mental spa for your thoughts. Use the questions above or create your own. Write what you want; your thoughts, emotions (whatever they are), your hopes, goals, and dreams. No one is going to judge you so don't judge yourself for whatever you are writing.

You can write about your athletic career, your personal life, your relationships, your failures and your successes. Use your journal to brainstorm about your current issues, keep track of training ideas and results, as well as to write out your rants and pose questions. Some days if you don't feel like writing out your thoughts with pen or pencil, just draw them out; and hey, if you want to use crayons or colored markers, go for it.

What you will discover is that when you read this journal weeks, months, or years from now, you will see your growth, your maturity, and your personal development. When you look back through the pages, you'll see how much progress you've made, what obstacles you've struggled with and overcome, and the life lessons you've learned along the way. It will all be in these pages so you can go back and reflect on how much you've grown as a person, an athlete, a son, a brother, a dad, a husband, a teammate, a friend.

Don't wait until tomorrow to start journaling. Start your first entry today!

"I like to think of goal setting as an important roadmap to one's destiny."

~ Adonal Foyle

QUOTE:

Date: _____

_____

_____

_____

_____

_____

_____

_____

_____

_____

_____

DRIVERS

QUOTE:

"I can shake off everything as I write; my sorrows disappear, my courage is reborn."

~ Anne Frank

Date: _____

_____

_____

_____

_____

_____

_____

_____

_____

_____

_____

_____

DRIVERS

QUOTE:

> "Documenting little details of your everyday life becomes a celebration of who you are."
>
> ~ Carolyn V. Hamilton

Date: _____

_____

_____

_____

_____

_____

_____

_____

_____

_____

_____

_____

DRIVERS

"Managing mental and physical skills AND emotions
are key fundamentals if an athlete wants
to excel in his sport."

~ Adonal Foyle

Date: _____

_____

_____

_____

_____

_____

_____

_____

_____

_____

_____

DRIVERS

QUOTE:

"Journaling is like whispering to one's self and listening at the same time."

~ Mina Murray

Date: _____

_____

_____

_____

_____

_____

_____

_____

_____

_____

_____

_____

DRIVERS

QUOTE:

"Writing in a journal each day allows you to direct your focus to what you accomplished, what you're grateful for, and what you're committed to doing better tomorrow. Thus, you more deeply enjoy your journey each day, feel good about any forward progress you've made, and use a heightened level of clarity to accelerate your results."

~ Hal Elrod

Date: _____

_____

_____

_____

_____

_____

_____

_____

_____

_____

_____

_____

DRIVERS

QUOTE:

"Harnessing one's emotions and releasing them at the appropriate time is a powerful weapon an athlete can possess in his quiver of opportunity."

~ Adonal Foyle

Date: _____

_____

_____

_____

_____

_____

_____

_____

_____

_____

_____

DRIVERS

QUOTE:

"Journaling is paying attention to the inside for the purpose of living well from the inside out."

~ Lee Wise

Date: _____

_____

_____

_____

_____

_____

_____

_____

_____

_____

_____

DRIVERS

QUOTE:

"Fill your paper with the breathings of your heart."

~ William Wordsworth

Date: _____

_____

_____

_____

_____

_____

_____

_____

_____

_____

_____

DRIVERS

QUOTE:

"Every athlete needs direction in their sport. They need a purpose, but more than that, they need a plan of action. I like to think of goal setting as an important roadmap to one's destiny."

~ Adonal Foyle

Date: _____

_____

_____

_____

_____

_____

_____

_____

_____

_____

_____

_____

DRIVERS

QUOTE:

"When I talk about goals, I refer to them as my direction, because if you don't have direction, you don't know where you're going to go."

~ Mark Munoz

Date: _____

_____

_____

_____

_____

_____

_____

_____

_____

_____

_____

DRIVERS

QUOTE:

"Journaling helps you to remember how strong you truly are within yourself."

~ Asad Meah

Date: _____

_____

_____

_____

_____

_____

_____

_____

_____

_____

_____

DRIVERS

DRIVERS

> "No building is better than its structural foundation, and no man (or woman) is better than his or her mental foundation."
>
> ~ John Wooden

Date: _____

_____

_____

_____

_____

_____

_____

_____

_____

_____

_____

_____

DRIVERS

QUOTE:

"Positive self-talk is when you engage in internal or external statements that are positive and that help build your confidence. Being positive in your thinking and being mindful of your thoughts can fuel you to be the best that you can be."

~ Adonal Foyle

Date: _____

_____

_____

_____

_____

_____

_____

_____

_____

_____

_____

_____

DRIVERS

QUOTE:

"Journal writing is a voyage to the interior."
~ Christina Baldwin

Date: _____

_____

_____

_____

_____

_____

_____

_____

_____

_____

_____

DRIVERS

QUOTE:

"Walking in integrity and finding your authentic self must include self-awareness. Self-awareness is about having an awareness of your character, feelings, motives, and desires."

~ Adonal Foyle

Date: _____

_____

_____

_____

_____

_____

_____

_____

_____

_____

_____

DRIVERS

QUOTE:

"The battle cry for every athlete is this: be forgetful about failure and never let circumstances undermine your confidence in your game."

~ **Adonal Foyle**

Date: _____

_____

_____

_____

_____

_____

_____

_____

_____

_____

_____

DRIVERS

QUOTE:

"The starting point of discovering who you are, your gifts, your talents, your dreams, is being comfortable with yourself. Spend time alone. Write in a journal."

~ Robin Sharma

Date: _____

_____

_____

_____

_____

_____

_____

_____

_____

_____

_____

DRIVERS

QUOTE:

"Finding your authentic self is about looking in places you often don't want to look."

~ Adonal Foyle

Date: _____

_____

_____

_____

_____

_____

_____

_____

_____

_____

_____

DRIVERS

QUOTE:

"The only thing I have done religiously in my life is keep a journal, I have hundreds of them, filled with feathers, flowers, photographs, and words – without locks, open on my shelves."

~ Terry Tempest Williams

Date: _____

_____

_____

_____

_____

_____

_____

_____

_____

_____

_____

_____

DRIVERS

Don't let your story stop here!
Keep writing…there are many
chapters of your life yet to be written.

DRIVERS
OF ATHLETIC SUCCESS

CPSIA information can be obtained
at www.ICGtesting.com
Printed in the USA
BVHW021246190122
626613BV00008B/412